If the garlic is too strong
And the tender chives too weak
If your onions make you cry
Take a Leek

Recipes: MAXINE J. SALTONSTALL
Illustrations: WAYNE MAYFIELD
Title Credit: VIRGINIA CARROLL

FIRST YOU TAKE A LEEK

Recipes with a Gourmet Touch

CHARLES E. TUTTLE COMPANY
Rutland, Vt. & Tokyo, Japan

Representatives

Continental Europe: BOXERBOOKS, INC., *Zurich*
British Isles: PRENTICE-HALL INTERNATIONAL, INC., *London*
Australasia: BOOK WISE (AUSTRALIA) PTY. LTD.
104-108 Sussex Street, Sydney 2000

Published by the Charles E. Tuttle Company, Inc.
of Rutland, Vermont & Tokyo, Japan
with editorial offices at
Suido 1-chome, 2-6, Bunkyo-ku, Tokyo, Japan

Copyright in Japan, 1969, by Charles E. Tuttle Co., Inc.

Library of Congress Catalog Card No. 70-94022

International Standard Book No. 0-8048-0748-5

First edition, 1969
Seventh printing, 1979

PRINTED IN JAPAN

CONTENTS

INTRODUCTION

ANY RELIABLE DICTIONARY will tell you this modest little vegetable is "closely allied to the onion," while on the other hand any reliable connoisseur of fine culinary tastes will tell you the leek is absolutely indispensable when aiming for subtlety of flavor in certain dishes.

For centuries the Welsh have given the leek credit for their great strength in battle, while Greeks, Egyptians and Romans have all, since ancient times, known of and served leeks in many ways, including the simple form of plain boiled with a butter or hollandaise sauce as we so often do with asparagus. They can also be braised, pureed, baked or stewed. So versatile are they, they are wonderful hot or cold—in puu puus*, soups, stews, salads, or you could even make a leek pie. Delicious.

*Hawaiian for canapes or hors d'oeuvres

To the new leek enthusiast let us remind you to use only the tender white part. The green tops would be tough and stringy, so be sure to trim both the tops and roots. The stalks should be crisp and firm and just as with its kissin' cousin, the scallion, the younger smaller stalks are naturally more tender and desirable. Right here I would have suggested "as with a woman" except for the fact that if you stood a leek and Twiggy side by side you couldn't tell the difference unless you bit into one. And we want to keep our similitudes along the well fed line.

And speaking of being well fed—let us get on with the recipes. I once had a sticker on my car that read "Made by broad A's in Boston"—so by the same token let me say here that the following recipes were concocted, offered, stolen and hoodwinked by and from my family and friends among whom you will find both broad and flat A's. But on the other hand, there is not one who will not agree with me that a little leek is a fine thing.

Leek and Split Pea Soup

Serves 6 eaters or 8 who just fool around!

Leeks, chopped—1/2 cup
Salt pork, diced—3 slices
Split peas, green, dried—1 lb
Onion, chopped—3/4 cup
Celery, chopped—1/2 cup
Ham bone or pig's knuckle—1
Sausage, knackwurst, or franks—1 lb
Bay leaf—1
Salt and pepper

Put the *split peas* in a colander and as you rinse them under cold running water pick out the imperfect ones. Put them in a good-sized pan. Now put the diced *salt pork* in the colander and pour some boiling water over it. Dry it off on a paper towel and then gently brown it in a skillet. To this add the chopped vegetables—*leeks*, *onion* and *celery* —and cook for about ten minutes. In the split pea pot, put the *ham bone* or the *pig's knuckle*, *bay leaf*, 2 teaspoons *salt*, ½ teaspoon *pepper*— freshly ground, black—and

$2\frac{1}{2}$ quarts of *cold water*. Cover and slowly bring to a boil. Don't let it boil hard because at this point you should remove the lid and skim off the top. Then back on with the lid and let it simmer for $2\frac{1}{2}$ hours. Take out the bay leaf and bones. Remove the ham from the bone and kind of pull it apart, or shred it; then set it aside. Put the split pea vegetable mixture through a food mill. Now all the ingredients go back into the pot and right here the seasoning is checked. Just check it—no fair eating a whole bowlful yet! Anyway, this is the time to add the sliced *knackwurst, sausage,* or *franks*—and let it cook for about ten minutes.

With garlic bread this is a winner.

And right here, let me tell you about garlic bread.........

Garlic Bread

GARLIC BREAD just ain't (in my opinion) unless it is done as taught to me by Randy Hall of Southampton, Long Island. I've known Randy for about thirty years and he's the only cook I know who can compete with my brother Don or my sister Louise Huff of Manhattan Beach, California. So, when he took over the making of garlic bread one evening to go along with the venison stew we were serving, I watched his every move.

I had always seen garlic bread made by almost slicing the sour dough French bread through, and then dabbing on a paste made of butter or margarine and garlic salt, then heating this mess in the oven with almost a tasteless result. This quickie ersatz method will no longer do. So try this:

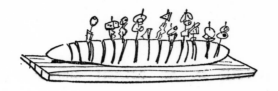

Peel several buttons of garlic and set them aside. Let your butter soften a little. Cut the bread in slices and place them under the broiler until one side is lightly toasted. Turn. Not you, the bread. Do not let the other side brown, but take it out when the bread is just a little rough. Now rub a piece of garlic lightly over the rough surface and the oil of the button will seep right into the bread. Butter the slices to the edges. I repeat, to the very edges of the bread because the crust is sheer ambrosia. Just before the bread is to be served, pop it under the broiler for a second and let it brown a little. There you have garlic bread!!

Put grated cheese on it if you like, or chives, or marshmallows for all I care (not really!), but do it right——it's worth it.

La Paloma Paella

THERE IS AS MUCH difference in Spanish and Mexican food as there are drops of water in the sea between the two countries. So when you visit Mexico don't come back and say you have liked or not liked the Spanish food because there isn't any. That is, unless you went to the one famous Spanish eating place in Mexico City, La Paloma, which I understand has been torn down.

While living in Cuernavaca, which is an hour's drive from the city, I had been told by so many friends of the La Paloma's wonderful Paella and also of their convivial atmosphere that I knew I had to make an effort to get there. Let me explain that once a gringo is settled in Cuernavaca, everything is an effort—and going to the city is an effort that sometimes has to be discussed and debated for weeks before the actual move takes place. If it takes place! But this time I was forced into it. I was doing some work for the Associated Press and was called into town by Charlie Guptill who was then head of AP for all of that territory —and I was summoned to his presence for a conference. For transportation I took a Turismo, which is a public limousine-type small bus—Mexican style. On the particular one I rode this day, was also one Amado Sylva Garcia, who resembled a scrubbed up Pancho Villa and was connected with the railroad in some vague way.

I had met Amado several times at as many parties and always enjoyed his company because he loved good music and made the best salad I ever ate. He had been asking to meet Charlie for a long time because he wanted to do some stories about the railroad—so I told him to meet us at La Paloma and we could have a good long talk

over a batch of Paella. Well, a Mexican is about as welcome in a Spanish restaurant as a bastard at a family reunion, but Amado decided to brave it—he was that eager. So we agreed to meet at 6. At 7, Charlie was still yelling at me so it was 7:30 before we got under way to rescue Amado.

The restaurant entrance led down a long, dark flight of stairs at the bottom of which was a rather large room with perhaps a dozen tables and no customers at all— except one—and you know who that was. Seven-thirty is hours too early for the evening meal in Mexico, so this gave all those loyal Spanish waiters plenty of time to put the hot eye on this interloper. Well—

poor Amado had had to have a little of the grape to steel his nerves. Matter of fact, he was smashed! Charlie caught the picture and wanting to make amends for our late arrival ordered two goatskins of wine (none for me, thanks!) and three orders of Paella and he and Amado were off and running. I might as well have been in Seattle for all the attention I was getting but figured it shouldn't be a total loss, so I ate Paella till I could hardly stand up. At 11 o'clock, which was when I left—alone—

they had the railroad running directly from Alaska to Acapulco (probably non-stop) and for all I know the "La Paloma" building was torn down with them still in it. Anyway the Paella was memorable, and the next time I ate it I was actually in Spain but under dramatically more conservative circumstances.

I give you the recipe and you may choose your own circumstances.

THIS RECIPE is for a mob so either invite in a bunch of demonstrators or cut it down to size. In either case you had better check your larder because some of these ingredients you just may not happen to have on hand.

Broilers, young, 2 to 3 lbs each—1 or 2
Shrimp, frozen or fresh—1/2 lb
Mussels—1 dozen
Lobster tails, each cracked in thirds—2
Chicken broth—2 cups
Chicken bouillon—1 cube
Peas, tiny fresh—1 lb; or frozen—1 package
Olive oil—1 cup

Garlic, minced—2 cloves
Sherry—1/4 cup
Bay leaf—1/2
Onion, chopped—1/4 cup
Leek, thinly sliced—1 cup
Tomatoes, canned—2 cups
Saffron—1 teaspoon
Rice—2 cups
Green pepper—1
Pimiento strips—1/4 cup

Have your butcher cut each chicken into about 8 pieces. Use the *necks*, *giblets*, bony parts of *backs* and tips of *wings* for the chicken broth. Cover them with *water*. Add about ½ teaspoon *salt*, ½ *onion*, a few *celery leaves* and let simmer, covered, for about 40 minutes. Strain and add the *bouillon cube*. If necessary, add a little *water* to make the necessary 2 full cups.

Scrub the *mussels* with a stiff brush under cold, running water and be sure you get out all the sand. If you find one that is open even a little bit give it the old heave-ho.

Shell the *shrimp* and cut out the black line down the back. Or easier, although not better, use frozen.

The perfect utensil in which to cook this is one of those Mexican or French earthenware casseroles. But most anything heavy and of a good size will do but it should be a handsome piece because it goes right to the table.

O.K. So heat the *olive oil* and gently brown the *chicken* in it. When it is not quite done take it out of the oil and set it aside. Add the *garlic* and *onion* and stir them around (preferably with a wooden spoon) until they are a golden color and then put in the *rice*. See that every grain gets a good oil bath and then put in the *broth, bay leaf, saffron, leek, sherry, peas, tomatoes,* and sliced *green pepper*. Give it a good stir adding about 2 teaspoons of salt. Now, carefully place the *chicken, shrimp, lobster,* and *mussels* in and around the rice so they look decorative in their various colors, and top it all with the *pimiento* strips. Cover and cook for no more than 30 minutes with the oven at 350 F.

Serve this with garlic bread and my favorite spinach salad and even those demonstrators will be happy.

Fresh Spinach Salad

THE FOLLOWING ANECDOTE is for adults only. Not because it is risque—I would say the only dirty thing that could result from this book is dishes—but, to recognize some of the characters in the cast one would have to be a little on the ripe side.

We are back in Cuernavaca. My roommate Betty Lockwood and I planned to give a costume party for someone's birthday whose name escapes me now. In those days ('48–'49) one could give a "gran fiesta" complete with all kinds of solid and liquid refreshments and a band of mariachis for about $20 American. That being the amount we had on hand we called everyone we knew in Cuernavaca and even imported a few from Mexico City. As the word spread it became *the* party and we were called by the local press for an item and guest list for their weekly "Social Activities" page. We were pretty tired of reading the same old guest lists week in and week

out so we set to work to spice ours up a bit with a few special guests interwoven among the legits.

How it ever got all the way into print without question we never knew, but once it hit the news stands we got calls from all over Mexico. Out "society" reporter never called us again—didn't even speak—but several hundred people got a good healthy laugh and there's nothing wrong with that.

Here is the guest list: Kels Elvins with

Bridie Murphy, Helen Fels, Leslie Van Dusen, Judge Crater, Mr. and Mrs. Ross Evans, Sr and Sra Edmundo Espino, Ambrose Bierce, Lili Saltonstall, Brooke Anderson, Dr and Mrs Roberto Quintero, Bret Harte, and on and on it went.

It completely spoiled me for ever giving a straight guest list again and recently when my daughter got married and I had to make out a list I could hardly restrain myself from throwing in maybe Peaches Browning, or would you believe—Sonny Tufts!

Anyway, the night of the party we had chiles rellenos (not those soggy cheese things). These took all day and were made by my cook Maria who filled the chiles with meat, raisins, and all kinds of wonderful things and then added the cheese sauce— they were so good you could hardly believe it—tacos, guacamole, chicken mole, garlic bread, numerous little things, and a big spinach salad.

Now over the years I have tried spinach salad in the few top restaurants around the country where it has been on the menu but they just don't get it quite right. The dressing is so simple I don't know where they go wrong—unless it is in the bacon. You must have good bacon. Here is how to do it:

First, only *you* can figure the amount of spinach to get. The spinach does not get cooked and shrink down so judge the servings as you would a lettuce salad—only with the spinach don't forget there will be no tomatoes or other vegetables to supplement it.

Buy the youngest, freshest spinach to be found and wash each leaf separately and thoroughly under cold running water. Pinch off the stems. If I am making for 6 or more I put the clean leaves in a pillow slip and throw in a few paper towels to absorb the moisture and after shaking it around a little it gets put in the refrigerator to stay perky.

Now, using only top grade bacon, cut up and cook 4 to 6 pieces until crisp, then drain them on a paper towel. When the grease has cooled a little pour it into a clean container (not in with your old bacon drippings). Wipe out the skillet with a paper towel, freeing it of all residue. Pour the fresh grease back into the pan. Be sure to get only the clear part of the grease. Right here I want to say I am sorry I cannot give you the exact measurement because it is all a matter of taste. So try this:

Keeping the drippings a little warm, add about a tablespoon of brown sugar and blend it in. Now slowly slosh in a few tablespoons of regular red wine vinegar—not garlic or tarragon or anything else—just regular red wine vinegar and blend it in. I always leave out a few of the spinach leaves and start dipping them in the sauce about now for testing. Under no circumstances let it get hot. This is not a wilted salad. Just fool around with it until you get it to your taste. There are only 3 ingredients to the sauce—bacon drippings, brown sugar, and red wine vinegar—anything added to it would spoil it.

If you have room on the pilot light, keep it there until ready for use, but don't put it on the spinach until just before serving.

This is great with ham or any other pork dish.

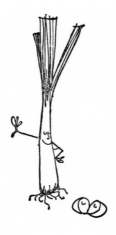

Leek Soup

Serves 4 big eaters or 6 *noshers*.

Leeks—6
Potatoes for boiling, medium-size—6
Parsley, chopped—1/2 cup
Butter or margarine—2 tablespoons
Egg yolk—1
Coffee cream—2 cups
Bacon—3 or 4 slices
Chicken broth or canned bouillon—6 cups
White onion—1
Nutmeg—optional

After washing the *leeks* and *parsley* thoroughly in cold water, chop the parsley and using only the white part of the leeks, cut them into little rounds. Peel and cube the *potatoes*. Peel and slice the *onion*. Have the *egg yolk* standing by in a small teacup or bowl. If you splash some cold water in the container and leave it wet, the egg yolk will not stick to the bottom or sides. Cut up the *bacon* and cook slowly—bacon should always be cooked slowly and turned often until it is crisp enough to crumble. Set aside to drain on a paper towel. Now take a pan that will hold at least 2 quarts and put

it over a medium low heat—adding 2 heaping tablespoons of *butter* or substitute. When the butter is melted, and don't let it brown, gently sauté the *leeks* and *onion*. Add the *broth* then the *parsley* and *potatoes*. Use a wooden spoon for stirring if you have one. When the potatoes are done take all the vegetables out of the liquid and strain and sieve them. Now you have a nice batch of puree, which would probably be great for the baby, but don't forget you're making soup for the whole family, so mix it back into the broth. This is a good time to add some plain or seasoned *salt* and *pepper*—to

taste. So many people forget to use white pepper and I think it would be very good in this. Remember the *egg yolk?* Mix a couple of sloshes of the stock with it and beat it a little before adding it to the pot. Now pour in the *cream* and keep stirring. Watch it closely so that it does not boil. If you think you would like a dash of *nutmeg*, now is the time to add it. Crumble the *bacon* on top of the individual servings.

I Love Cabbage— But—

ALONG THE COSTA DEL SOL, between Malaga and Algeciras in Spain, will be found some of the most beautiful and picturesque stretches of scenery in the world. You get the full treatment—on your left the blue Mediterranean surf lapping at your heels along the way and on your right the ancient verdant rolling hills dotted here and there with an old old fort, and straight ahead as you near your goal you can see the higher plains of Africa—almost as a beckoning mirage.

Even as viewed from a questionably modern bus the unfolding panorama was always so

lovely I half expected to hear the assistant
director yell, "Strike the set—take it away
—everybody back at 7 tomorrow," and see
it all disappear on a big truck.

But you do get to Algeciras and if your
timing has been right you will see at the
dock a ship that could be compared with a
good sized river boat taking on passengers
bound for Tangier. Just as some people's
imaginations run to seasickness at the
sight of a ship—mine goes about face, and
I allow as how I am hungry. Half starved in
fact. So before I even get a good deck chair
I am off to view the dining room.

Have you ever been on the leeward side of
a paper mill—a glue factory—a stock yard?
On my first trip to Tangier I thought I had
boarded an old slave ship or a cattle boat,
because even before my feet touched the

deck I could smell it. I hurried on—imagining untold horrors in the hold—only to find that the closer I got to the dining room and galley the more my nostrils were offended. Well, my dears, these were cooking odors from the lunch that we were about to be served. It was a chicken and cabbage combination that had been boiled since the ship was launched, and what it had been boiled in boggled my thoughts so badly that I ate nothing but rolls, celery, and radishes.

It was a rough voyage, and it was quite some time before I could present at my own table cabbage prepared in my own way and taught to me by my dear old Mom.

Cabbage Supreme

NO MATTER IF I have cabbage cooked or in slaw, I always first cut it in half and soak it in cold salted water. Drain. Coarsely chop. Wash and thinly slice *2 leeks*—depending upon their size and the amount of cabbage used. Gently fry *3* or *4* strips of *bacon* in a large skillet until crisp, then set them aside on a paper towel. Put the chopped *cabbage* in the skillet with the bacon drippings. Note: If you have an excess of fat, drain a little of it off. Mix in the *leek* slices, season with just a little seasoned *salt*, black *pepper*, enough water to form a little steam, cover and cook for *5* or *6* minutes.

I don't like any of my vegetables cooked beyond taste and recognition and I am sure you will enjoy this more if it is not over-done. Just before serving, crumble the *bacon* and sprinkle it over the top. This is cabbage supreme.

One of my other very favorite forms of cabbage is in a slaw. My dictionary gives the definition of cole slaw as "a salad of sliced cabbage." It does not go on to say "or any variation thereof"—and this is a point I have been trying to make for years—if one adds pineapple or carrot or green pepper or any other fruit or vegetable, then it is no longer cole slaw—it has become a cabbage and pineapple or cabbage and carrot or cabbage and whatever else, salad.

You know the old maxim that goes "No matter how you slice it, it's still baloney." Well, the same does not hold for cole slaw.

All my life I have liked it and could have eaten it twice a day every day, but could never seem to make it properly. I grated and chopped and seasoned and tested over and over again, but I just didn't get it. So, when shortly after I came to live in Honolulu I was invited to dinner at one Suzanne Teller's apartment and she produced a slaw the likes of which I had given up hopes of ever finding. I could hardly believe my little taste buds. They were throbbing and bobbing and clamouring for more and you can believe I did not leave there without the recipe.

Since that time 2 years ago, I have made as much cole slaw as Reuben's in New York— and although mine is still not up to Suzanne's —here is her recipe—and rots o'ruck!!

Suzanne's Slaw

USE A SMALL solid head of cabbage or ½ of a large one. In any case soak it, cut side down, in ice cold salted water for at least 15 minutes before slicing. Suzanne uses a big French chopping knife but if you don't have one, any good sharp knife will do.

Slice, or rather, shave down the cut side of one of the halves to make fine shreds. Now add all the ingredients listed below except the paprika—which is used only as a garnish. Refrigerate until ready to serve.

Suzanne says the secret of her slaw is—it has to be very very cold, tart, and have lots of mayonnaise.

Canned milk—3 tablespoons
Cider vinegar—3 or 4 tablespoons
Leek, minced—1
Parsley, minced—3 or 4 sprigs
Salt and pepper
Sugar—a sprinkle
Lemon—a squeeze
Paprika—a dash

Calcium Carbonate
with Lactose

I HAVE HAD some pretty funny experiences involving food—two come to mind very quickly.

It was a Sunday afternoon in Spain and I was visiting a rather elderly couple who had decided to retire from the mad pace of the United States and settle down in Torremolinos. Torremolinos! That's like choosing Las Vegas over Reno for a rest cure. Nevertheless on this particular day, about 20 other assorted types also called on my

friends and one of them brought in—
freshly caught—at least 50 tiny sardine-
like fish that had to be cooked immediately.
I was on. First I washed the fish and put the
cooking oil on to heat in a large skillet.
Next the fish were dipped in beaten egg,
then flour, and then popped into the hot oil.
Well sir, they never browned or crisped up
or any thing, like they had always done
before and even worse they tasted like wet
suede gloves. But then, I had never before
inadvertently substituted calcium carbonate
with lactose for flour either!

In my home the canister marked "flour" contains flour and altho I still don't know a great deal about calcium carbonate with lactose, I can say definitely that it is not advisable to use it in any form of cookery and should under no circumstances be kept on the kitchen shelf.

Very Hot Ham

THE OTHER INCIDENT involves a ham. Altho friends were involved, the ham was of the baking variety. This was in the home of the Hollywood director, William Witney, and his wife Maxine. (She was formerly known as Maxine Doyle). Dinner was running late, Maxine had this glazed ham sitting on top of the oven, and she asked Billy to please put it on a platter while she assembled the other last minute dishes. Dr. Richard Walt was standing with his back to the sink and another director, John English, was leaning against the kitchen table. I came through the door as the ham went flying over my head in the neatest Tinkers, Evers to Chance, 3-way toss since the original. After I picked a few cloves out of my hair, I learned that Billy had lost control of the ham half way between the roaster and the platter and rather than let it hit the floor, he had made a plunge for it —and caught it. Well, you just can't stand around holding a hot ham so of course you forward pass it to a friend. A few cloves were lost and all the pineapple slices, but it was a scrumptious ham—and I have often wondered since if it was the excitement of that dinner that inspired Billy to invest in a highly successful hog farm which produces such fine pork that it is bought by Farmer John. But enough of these stories. From here on you are going to get some really fine recipes—and if you want to go throwing things around—my advice to you is—cool it.

Leeks in Butter Sauce

LEE SALTONSTALL WOOLAWAY

Recipe for 4

Leeks, young and tender—1 lb
Butter or margarine—1/4 cup
Onion, chopped—1 tablespoon
Flour—1 tablespoon
Parsley, finely chopped—1/2 tablespoon

Thoroughly wash the *leeks* and trim as previously suggested (page 9). Lay them out in a large skillet and add 1 cup of *water*. When they come to a boil reduce the heat and simmer, covered, until tender. Watch them carefully because this will take less than 10 minutes. Drain but save the liquid—should be about ¾ cup. Place the leeks on a serving platter and keep warm. Sauté the chopped *onion* in the *butter* or margarine for about 4 or 5 minutes and then blend in the flour. Gradually add the reserved liquid and bring to a soft boil, stirring constantly. Pour this over the leeks and garnish with the chopped parsley.

This is delicious with pork chops, ham or even veal.

Leeks au Gratin

MARYLOU ESTRADA

THIS ORIGINAL RECIPE called for two bunches of leeks and claimed to feed 8, but I think it would depend on how many leeks come in a bunch in your market—and also how heavy your meat dish is and/or what your other vegetable will be. You will just have to use good judgment—but I do hope you try it because it really is very good.

All you need to get are enough leeks to make approximately 4 lbs (or a little less) and some good nippy cheese to grate (enough for one cup) or buy some already grated.

Wash and trim the leeks as we have described before (page 9). Cover them with salted water and boil until tender (about 10 minutes). Drain thoroughly and arrange in a buttered baking dish. Sprinkle the grated cheese and pepper to taste over the top and pop it under the broiler until the cheese is melted. Watch it closely.

This is great with either meat loaf or chicken.

Chicken-with-Leeks Casserole

Serves 4 if nobody's watching TV—or 6 if there's a good show on and nobody's paying attention anyway.

Stewing chicken—1
Leeks—4
Celery—3 large or 4 smaller stalks
Carrots—4
Onions—2
Bay leaf—1
Chicken bouillon cube—1
Butter or substitute
Cloves
Thyme
Lemon
Chives
Sauterne, very dry—small bottle

Heat oven to 350 F. If your *chicken* is not already cut up, you can cook it whole and carve it after it is done. But cut or whole, rub it thoroughly with *lemon* and let it set for a few minutes. Put it in a dutch-oven or similar container that has a good tight cover and add 2 cups of cold *water*. Place it over a medium-low burner. Now slice the *leeks* (white parts only), and the *onions*, *celery*, and *carrots* and sauté them together slowly in 2 heaping tablespoons of *butter* or margarine until the leeks turn golden. They are more delicate than the other vegetables so watch them closely.

When the chicken has started to boil slowly add the sautéed vegetables, *cloves* (4), *salt*, *pepper*, and 1 chicken *bouillon cube*. Easy on the salt because of the B. cube. Pour about 1 cup of the *sauterne* over it all and get the cover on good and tight. Cook for about 2 hours in a 350° oven. If you have cooked the chicken whole, take it out of the liquid now and carve it. In any case put it in a warm tureen or casserole dish. Add the remaining cup of sauterne to the broth, correct the seasoning to taste, and reheat. Pour the liquid over the chicken, sprinkle some chopped chives over the top and fall to. Real good!!

Vichyssoise with Curry

A SUMPTUOUS elegant-tasting dish. Impress your husband's boss with this one—or your best beau—or better yet your whole family. It mut be partially made the day before you plan to serve it and requires plenty of TLC* The recipe is for 8 servings so cut down or add to as need be.

Who doesn't know that's "Tender Loving Care"?

Leeks—1 doz
Butter—1/4 cup
Cream of chicken soup, condensed—1 can
Curry powder—1 teaspoon
Sour cream—2 cups
Sauterne, dry—1/4 cup
Potatoes, medium-size—4
Cream—1 cup
White pepper
Half 'n half—2 cups
Chives, finely chopped—1 bunch

First boil, peel, and dice the *potatoes*. Then after the *leeks* have been washed and trimmed, slice them very thin. Use a saucepan worthy of such a dish and in it melt the *butter* and gently sauté the leeks for about 10 minutes. You certainly know by now that they should never get brown—only golden. Add the cream of *chicken soup*, the *sauterne*, and simmer for 20 minutes. Now it is time for the *potatoes* and *cream*, and another 10 minutes of simmering. Strain into another pan and force the solids through a sieve. Toss in 2 teaspoons *salt*, ¼ teaspoon *white pepper*, the *curry powder* and 1 cup of the *half 'n' half*. Stir the mixture thoroughly with a wooden spoon—if you have one.

You're going to put the soup in the refrigerator overnight so let it cool first. A couple of hours before you are ready to serve—have the soup bowls chilling. Add the *sour cream* and the other cup of *half 'n half* to the mixture and keep it good and cold. The chopped *chives* are the garnish.

This is almost better than Fresca!

Potato–Leek Soup

Mrs Michael Ross

EVERY TIME my eye catches this recipe I can picture the falling snow and the kids outside falling right along with it and in it —and how hungry they will be when they come in. What better than this hot sturdy soup with crispy croutons floating on top. A wonderful lunch dish for them—and you! If there are more than 4 of you increase the recipe.

Leeks, sliced—1 cup
Water, cold—4 cups
Bay leaf—1
Celery, chopped—1/4 cup
Parsley, minced—2 tablespoons
Salt—1 teaspoon
Croutons
Onion, grated—1/2 small one
Milk—1 cup
Butter or margarine—3 tablespoons
Chili sauce or catsup—2 tablespoons
Potatoes, medium-size, diced—2

Melt the butter and lightly cook the *leeks*.
Add *water, bay leaf,* and *chili sauce.* Simmer
for 20 minutes—covered, and then put in
all the *other ingredients* except the milk.
When the potatoes are done, add the *milk*
and only let it get hot—do not let it boil.
Croutons with a slight touch of garlic flavor
are especially good with this.

Sis's Fishes

AND SO LET US bring to a close our suggestions of gastronomic goodies with a fish dish that is a real humdinger.

You are forthwith warned that this is a "scales be damned" dish (pun intended), so if the contents of your table are hampered by such stuff and nonsense as a caloric count, proceed no further. Otherwise either bait your hook or go in all haste to your favorite fish market and get 2 lbs (or a little less) of halibut or sole cut ¾ inch thick.

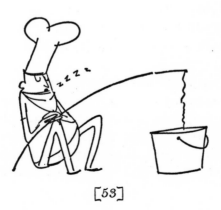

Cream of shrimp soup, frozen—1 can
Sour cream—1 small carton
Leek—1; or scallions (green onions)—3
Shrimp, tiny—1 smallest can
Lime juice—1/3 cup
Butter or margarine, melted—1/4 cup
Marjoram—pinch
Black pepper, ground
Garlic powder
Salt, seasoned

Marinate *fillets* in the *lime juice* for ½ hour—
turning often. Discard juice and place fish
on a broiler pan. Dot filets with the *butter* or
margarine and season with *garlic* and
seasoned *salt*. Broil under a medium low
heat for about 6 minutes on each side and
baste 2 or 3 times. Now place them in a
casserole. Mix and heat the *soup* and *sour
cream* slowly and pour it over the filets.
Bake in a 325 F. oven for ½ hour—only.

As this is baking—chop the *scallions* (little
green onions) or thinly slice the *leek* and
then only warm them or it and the tiny
shrimp in the skillet in which you melted the
butter. I repeat, only keep this warm—do
not let it cook. This is used as a garnish and

truly adds the gourmet touch to this remarkable dish.

You might as well "let it all hang out" as the hippies say and get some of those flakey baking powder biscuits (not the frozen) that would be found in the refrigerator department.

Of all the dishes of fishes I have, this just about tops them all.

So—in conclusion—may I ask——

Now that you've had your Leek Don't you feel better?

TIPS

1. An excellent sauce for ham: Heat 1 jar of French mustard and 1 jar of current jelly in the top of a double boiler.

2. Moisten meat stuffing with a cup of buttermilk.

3. Add a little Coca-Cola or beer to pot roast for gravy.

4. Put a little nippy cheese in meat loaf.

5. If cucumber is bitter, cut both ends and rub each end with the cut piece. Rinse.

6. Quick way to press garlic: Place pealed cloves of garlic between folds of wax paper and press with wooden spoon. Sure beats cleaning the garlic press.

ABOUT
THE AUTHOR

MAXINE J. SALTONSTALL, winner of swimming medals and beauty contests, first met her good friend Virginia Carroll (the one solely responsible for making this gourmet gag) when they appeared in the Astaire-Rogers film *Roberta*, years ago.

Mrs. Saltonstall has had a most varied career in the fields of entertainment, the arts, and journalism, succeeding very nicely in doing well just about whatever she had a mind to do.

Although she studied at the Sorbonne, Paris, and at Mexico City College, she admits: "I was never graduated from any school of higher education although I am always attending classes. There have been special courses in Business Administration,

Spanish, Hula, Investments, Chemistry, Semantics, Politics, and so many others I can no longer recall.

"Bridge clubs, drinking bouts (known in some circles as cocktail parties) and *all* clubby little get-togethers are the very nadir of existence to me—so, one could say, I am not a joiner. I learned this lesson in New York where I was living during most of W.W. II. In my wild anxiety to do anything to help, I offered myself and all my youthful eagerness to a women's volunteer group. Well, sir, that was short-lived because until they found I had a Park Avenue address I couldn't even get in to roll bandages—but after I was properly pigeon-holed I was considered just the one to transport visiting Pentagon Brass from perhaps the Stork Club to some other equally vital point. They were told they could take their organization and their visiting Brass and shove them all the way up Park Avenue, and I returned to Washington, D.C. to continue hounding the Red Cross for news of my brother who had been taken POW on Corregidor.

"I suppose much more 'stuff' could be dredged up out of my past but I move pretty

fast and the wake that I leave behind me sweeps the memory all but clean."

She has a very attractive married daughter who frequently appears in television commercials and is active in presenting fashion shows.

Wayne Mayfield, who drew the delightful sketches for this book, is a member of the very successful Hawaiian firm of Mayfield, Smith, Park & Ruckert Advertising, Inc.